123

SESAME STREET®

Go Green with Sesame Street

IT'S EARTH DAY, COOKIE MONSTER!

Mary Lindeen

Lerner Publications ◆ Minneapolis

Cooperating and sharing are an important part of *Sesame Street*—and of taking care of our planet. We all share Earth, so it's up to all of us to take care of it together. The *Go Green with Sesame Street*® books cover everything from appreciating Earth's beauty, to conserving its resources, to helping keep it clean, and more. And the familiar, furry friends from *Sesame Street* offer young readers some easy ways to help protect their planet.

Sincerely,

The Editors at Sesame Workshop

The text of this book is printed on paper that is made with 30 percent recycled postconsumer waste fibers.

Table of Contents

Home Sweet Home

Planet Earth home to every person, animal, and, most important, MONSTER.

We can all work together to take care of Earth!

Our Amazing Earth

Earth is a special place. From space, it looks like a big blue-and-green ball.

Earth look like big blue cookie to me!

Earth gives all creatures places to live and air to breathe.

Every day we can enjoy Earth.
We can go for walks or play outside.

The First Earth Day

A man named Gaylord Nelson wanted people to celebrate Earth.

Mr. Nelson was a US senator from the state of Wisconsin.

Mr. Nelson thought everyone should take care of Earth!

13

Senator Nelson organized the first Earth Day. Earth Day happens on April 22.

Yay, Earth Day!
Me love to celebrate!

Soon people around the world began to celebrate Earth Day.

Earth Day Celebrations

People celebrate Earth Day in different ways.
Some people have parades.

I will count the people: 1, 2, 3 . . .

You got lot of counting to do. So many people love Earth!

Kids recycle to make colorful pictures. The art reminds people to take care of Earth.

19

Some people plant gardens. Plants give us food and help keep the air clean. Plants are good for Earth.

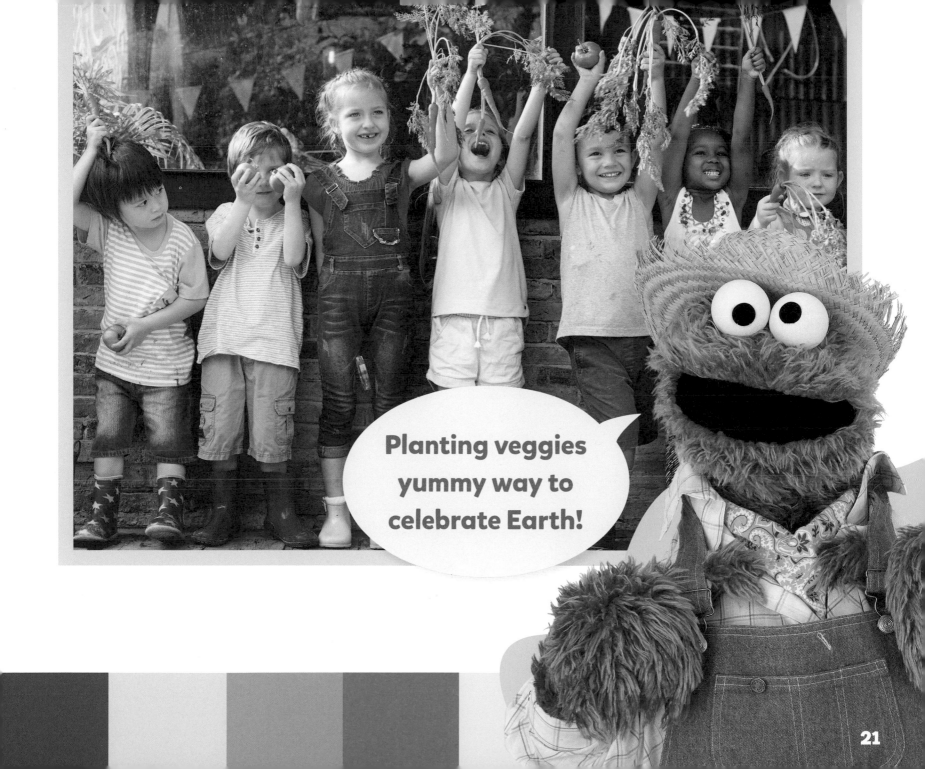

Many people help clean up Earth. They pick up trash at parks, beaches, and streams.

Come on, Oscar, you'll love this! Let's go pick up trash!

Cleaning up helps keep Earth healthy.

23

When we celebrate Earth Day, we celebrate our home. We work to make it a better place to live.

Which Earth Day
idea is your favorite?
How could *you*
celebrate Earth Day?

Earth Day Every Day

Every day is a good day to celebrate Earth! Here's how you can help:

- Put trash where it belongs.

- Plant flowers, trees, or vegetables.

- Recycle paper, plastics, and glass. What else can you recycle?

- For short trips, how about walking or biking instead of riding in a car?

A Wonder-Full Walk

Make your own art with the wonders you find on a walk!

1. Go for a family walk outdoors.

2. Collect things such as twigs, leaves, and acorns for your art project. But be careful! Don't touch things you don't know about, and use only things already on the ground.

3. When you get home, spread out your collection. Make a beautiful picture!

Glossary

celebrate: to honor in a special way

creature: a person, animal, or monster

organized: planned out

recycle: to reuse something in a different way

For Benjamin, who makes Earth a better place to be every single day

Index

Photo Acknowledgments

Additional image credits: vectortatu/Shutterstock.com, throughout (background); Hero Images/Getty Images, pp. 5, 10; Vitalij Cerepok/EyeEm/Getty Images, p. 7; Tim Melling/Getty Images, p. 8; andrew Wood/Getty Images, p. 9; Dubicki Photography/Getty Images, p. 11; Idaho Statesman/Getty Images, p. 12; FatCamera/Getty Images, pp. 13, 24, 29; Sergei Bachlakov/Shutterstock.com, p. 15; Michael Wheatley/Alamy Stock Photo, p. 17; Inna Reznik /Shutterstock.com, p. 18; tchara/Getty Images, p. 19; fstop123/Getty Images, p. 20; Rawpixel.com/Shutterstock.com, p. 21; hedgehog94/Shutterstock.com, p. 23; Brandon Tabiolo/Getty Images, p. 26; MortenChr/Getty Images, p. 30.
Cover: neur0tix/Shutterstock.com (background); Galyna_P/Shutterstock.com (world).

Lerner Publications Company
An imprint of Lerner Publishing Group, Inc.
241 First Avenue North
Minneapolis, MN 55401 USA

For reading levels and more information, look up this title at www.lernerbooks.com.

Main body text set in Mikado.
Typeface provided by HVD.

Library of Congress Cataloging-in-Publication Data

Names: Lindeen, Mary author. | Children's Television Workshop.
Title: It's Earth Day, Cookie Monster! / Mary Lindeen.
Other titles: Sesame Street (Television program)
Description: Minneapolis : Lerner Publications, [2020] | Series: Go green with Sesame Street | Includes index. | Audience: Ages: 4-8. | Audience: Grades: K to Grade 3.
Identifiers: LCCN 2019011155 (print) | LCCN 2019014589 (ebook) | ISBN 9781541572607 (library binding : alk. paper) | ISBN 9781541583092 (eb pdf)
Subjects: LCSH: Earth Day—Juvenile literature. | Cookie Monster (Fictitious character)—Juvenile literature.
Classification: LCC GE195.5 .L564 2020 (print) | LCC GE195.5 (ebook) | DDC 394.262—dc23

LC record available at https://lccn.loc.gov/2019011155
LC ebook record available at https://lccn.loc.gov/2019014589

Manufactured in the United States of America
1-46527-47572-6/25/2019